Sometimes He Buys Me Grapes

Sometimes He Buys Me Grapes

A MEMOIR
SONG AND DANCE OF LIFE

REGINA GALE

RG

RG PUBLISHING

This book is a work based on the author's perception of her experiences in her life. Any resemblance to actual persons, living or dead, events, or locales is her reaction to what she lived and perceived to be fact.

RG Books are published by
RG Publishing
North Carolina
Copyright © 2016 by Regina Gale

For information contact:
FiFi@sometimeshebuysmegrapes.com
http://www.sometimeshebuysmegrapes.com

Book and Cover design by Nathaniel Dasco
ISBN: 978-0-9976495-0-5 paperback
Library of Congress Control Number: 2016910765
First Edition: July 2016

10 9 8 7 6 5 4 3 2 1

DEDICATION

This book is dedicated to my son, CJ.

CJ, with your birth I became more intentional with my actions as I considered the responsibility awarded to me with the gift of your life. Your belief in me inspires me to keep reaching as I want you to also do.

For 10 years I prayed earnestly to have a child, I never gave up hope. I believed a miracle could happen. It did. I was blessed with you.

I still believe in miracles.

TABLE OF CONTENTS

SPECIAL BONUS GIFT FROM
REGINA GALE

Now that you have your copy of *Sometimes He Buys Me Grapes*, you can enjoy the ongoing conversation and dialogue that centers on relationships with people you love and care about.

The language is candid, real and live. It allows you the opportunity to look at your own situation with different eyes. This will help you attain the most positive relationships you can have for yourself, which will absolutely impact all the people you care about.

The conversation continues with a free gift for you.

Reflections of Love, a chapbook, is offered for sale but **is a special gift to you.** Go to http://www.sometimeshebuysmegrapes.com/ROLbook to register for your gift. As another bonus, *you will automatically be added to my newsletter list. You may unsubscribe at any time.*

Identifying how and what you feel in your relationships allows you to improve them and improve the quality of your life.

Always,

Regina Gale

WHAT'S IMPORTANT

The memories and emotions I share within the pages of this book is divided into seven sections.

Family

Friends

Desire

Love

The Break-up

Moving on

Back to Me

This memoir is about relationships and what happens with them when you are in them. It reveals a very candid look at how, over time, I have treated myself and others and how others have treated me. There are no secrets left imagined as the emotions expressed remind one that our relationship with each other as people is more important than anything else.

It is intimate and personal... and it is also about you.

FAMILY

A MESSAGE TO MY SON

As your mother, each time I look at you I see nothing but love. You have been the best gift I have ever received. I call you a gift but in reality, I was given the privilege to nurture you and protect you. I was given charge to direct you during your formative years, so that you may find your destiny and know that it is yours.

I have learned to parent through trial and error. Your showing up in this world took that selfish person I was and made me selfless in many respects. It was amazing how all of a sudden, even before you were born, I started to portray this "motherly" instinct that made me want to protect you 24/7. Your future became a concern immediately, and all I can say is yes, I have made many mistakes, but I always did the best that I could at any particular time.

Today, the gift I give to you freely is validation from me of who you are, as a man. You are a good man.

Even though you are still young and finding your place in the world, I am very proud of what I see. As you go forward, I will continue to fight for your future and protect you in ways that all mothers do for their children. But of course it will look very different, because now you are a young man and not a child. I will not run to pick you up and "fix" things every time you fall. I will be standing on the sidelines cheering you on, often quietly, as you step closer toward assuming the responsibilities that come with manhood.

I smile when I think about the things you are. You are kind, you are thoughtful and you are smart. There is no one else like you. I admire how you are flexible enough to consider that you don't know all the things you think you know. More than that, you are respectful to me, your mother and to others, and you love God.

Every child is born through a woman. You must remember that as a man. A woman presented you to the world. You will be that present to some woman one day, and she will be your cherished gift who you will honor. Who knows, one day, your woman may present you with a gift of life from your seed, because every child is born of a woman.

Before that time, I must share some things with you so that you can show up as the man she deserves.

It is easier for a woman to love a man who loves her well. My son, I want you to love her well so that she will be unable to do anything but love you back.

Remember these things:

- Having male parts does not make you a man. It makes you male.
- A real man understands that when he shows love to the woman from whom his seed has sprung, all will be well.
- Providing the seed that impregnates a woman does not make you a man. A real man cultivates that seed every step of the way during the growth of the life that has come into being. You have to always show up.
- A real man understands hearing the word daddy, is one of the greatest gifts and sweetest songs he will ever hear.
- A real man can be vulnerable when it comes to showing his dedication and devotion for those he loves and has been given responsibility for.

- A real man will come to understand that his woman needs intimacy, which is not always sex.
- A real man figures out how to communicate with his mate whom he sometimes has to admit he does not understand. Keep trying, the benefits will be so rewarding.
- A real man fosters a strong sense of security with his mate and the rest of the family.
- A real man takes responsibility for those things around him, without having to always be in control.
- There will be times when you will not feel strong, but your woman will then be there for you and will not let anything hurt you, if she has no doubt that you love her, as your cherished woman.

With everything I have said, up to this point you must never forget that a real man is a whole human being before and during his relationship.

It is important to enjoy your hobbies, spend time with friends who only want the best for you, and enjoy plenty of good food. This you must hold on to because when you are happy, happiness will follow you were ever you go.

All of this may seem like a tall order, but it really is not.
It will enhance your ability to love.

You are a good man.

I love you, be safe, stay strong,
Mom

DON'T BE AFRAID

To my son
To my nieces
To my nephews,
To hearts of my heart
My mantra has always been
Don't be afraid

I even had to step up the game
Of my own life
In order to give meaning
To the example
I would be
In their lives

As they looked to me to see
If I did as I asked of them,
Don't be afraid

I now tell myself every day
Don't be afraid

Just be
Just do
And I will be
What I want them to see

Don't be afraid

FAMILY

At least once a year
My eyes are opened to
The history of my life

The family time together
Shares the wealth of all the treasures
Of the many smiling faces
That reminds us of each other

From the kitchen
To the dining room
To the family room
And back to the kitchen
We reminisce about the years gone by
Daring to share our future dreams
Dropping all walls as we bared our souls
With people who really care
About me
And you
And we
All the people we love
The family

Divulging facts that have remained unsaid
For much too long
But time now allows some truths to come to light
And the family gathers near
Not just to hear
But to heal
The only way family can

We laugh,
We cry
We break bread
And say
This is the way we survive
Together
Gathered
As one family
With many extensions
But as one

I look forward
To time
That comes at least
Once a year

FAMILY

The wealth of all the treasures
In the many smiling faces
That reminds us of
Mom and Dad and love

HE SMELLED SO GOOD

I was probably around 6 or 7 years old when I first realized that men could smell delightful. I have never forgotten that spicy cinnamon fragrance that came out of that oddly shaped bottle of after shave my father would use after he shaved the stubble that had grown on his face overnight.

How I looked forward to catching daddy in the act of shaving. I considered it our special bonding time and I did my best to be a part of his ritual as often I as I could.

Whenever I would see him heading toward the bathroom with his shaving gear, which he kept safely out of reach of his curious children, I would dash in the bathroom and stand by his side and ask could I watch him shave. I'd promise I would be quiet and not talk a lot...which he always chuckled at, and would then say "ok baby girl." We both knew that I was lying.

As the ritual began, I would immediately ask, if I could dip the shaving brush into the fluffy white foam in the cup. When he said yes, as he often did, I would stir the shaving cream round and round and then scoop some of the foam on my hands as I handed daddy his shaving brush. I would play with this foamy shaving cream while watching daddy's stubbly hairy face become baby soft smooth. I often asked to feel his face before he shaved and then after he shaved, and then began chattering about the noticeable difference, and how it felt to my fingers.

This primary activity was fun to watch and I was a great "helper." But for me, the best part was after he shaved. Daddy would reach for that oddly shaped bottle with his left hand, and twist the cap off of the bottle with his right hand. Then, he would place the cap on the side of the sink, and simultaneously transfer the bottle into his right hand and turn it slightly upside down and sprinkle some of the liquid in the bottle into his left hand. He would then put the bottle down on the sink and slightly rub his hands together. He would then open his hands up and gently pat the liquid that was on his hands onto his face.

I would be giggling with delight during this ritual, partly because daddy made it fun for me but the spicy scent that emerged from that bottle smelled so good. I would often blurt out," daddy, you smell so good!!!"

Little did my father know that those times would be "special moments" in my life. It evokes all the things I thought were good in a man (my dad) at that time. He was strong, kind, funny, playful, stern, dedicated and at times a strict disciplinarian. There was never any doubt that he loved his wife and kids.

So now, whenever my senses get a whiff that is similar to that "unnamed aftershave," I cannot help but remember sharing special moments that are now a memory of a loving man that was my father. I also remember that he smelled so good.

I AM NOT THAT GIRL

He gave me a kiss on the cheek
As he picked up his keys
And said to me
I will be back in a bit

We smiled at each other
As he opened the door
I thought to myself
I am such a lucky girl
How I love him
With all of my heart
And I think that he is such a sweet heart

It got very late
My head began to ache
As I worried where on earth
My sweetie pie was
He said he would be back in a bit
And I don't want to fret
So instead, I began walking and pacing the floor

I decided to send him a text
Asking where are you at?

As I started to send it
My finger intentionally missed it
Then without hesitation
I hit delete instead
My brain said chill out
The man needs some space
And you need time to contemplate

So many things have changed between us
I feel it
I know it
There is someone new
In his heart and I am feeling blue
Time flew by so fast
That I did not really consider
That me,
The one who loves him so much
Would have to admit to myself that
I am not that girl

My baby boy is no longer my baby
He is now a young man
And I am not that girl
Who is the center of his world

I am not that girl
That makes his eyes sparkle
The one that makes him feel as powerful as superman
The one who is number one in his heart

I smiled and I remembered my youth
And I said to myself,
I will never again be that girl for him
No, I am not that girl

He gave me a kiss on the cheek
As he picked up his keys
And said to me
I will be back in a bit

MY FIRST TRUE GIRLFRIEND

That special woman
had my trust.
She knew my secrets
And cared about my feelings.
Her expressions of sincerity
Her powerful examples of responsibility
Shaped what became the relationship
With my first true girlfriend.

As people come and go in life
She was always there
Enforcing a bond that we shared
Giving validation as needed
Unwavering support pushing me
Willing to correct lovingly
She gave meaning to what
A girlfriend should be

Allowing me to shine
Taught me how to be a light so others could see
When misunderstandings bruised my self-image

She showed how actions of love
Cures any hurt feelings

Enabling me to grow to be better
Even when I could not see how to move forward
When I felt backed up against a door
She taught me keys that would open any lock
She was a gift to my life
My first true girlfriend was that to me

I was 20 something
When I realized that
The woman I had always referred to as mom
Was the best girlfriend I would ever have
She inspired me with words of wisdom
Cherished me and showed me how precious
I was to her.
Demanding that I figure out who I am
So that I could fully experience a happy life
Which is what she wanted for me.
I honor her even to this day

She was my first girlfriend
She was a true girlfriend
She was my first true girlfriend
And I called her mom.

MY MOTHER PRAYED FOR ME

My mother prayed for me
She prayed that I'd be strong
So that I could carry on,
When everyone was gone

Because she cared for me
And wanted me to be free
To be the best of me
And now I clearly see

That it takes time to be
A person who can really be free
Because now I understand
Things happened I could not plan

Oh yes my mother prayed for me
And someone prayed for you to be
The awesome individual
you turned out to be.

NOT LIKE MY MOTHER

When I was young I swore I did not want to be anything like my mother. She was wonderful, but she was, after all, my mother.

I adored her as a woman. She was my role model.

She was beautiful on the inside and out. She was kind, and she always made time to do for others. She was a teacher and a friend. But, she was just my mother.

She happened to be the wisest woman I knew, and I always felt free to confide in her...no matter what. And as funny as it seems, she always believed in me.

I clearly hear her prophetic words, "One of these days, you will understand what I am talking about." I grew to love her more and more as I aged.

There was a certain kind of wisdom that I acquired once I left the comfort, rules, love and care of home. For as smart as I thought I was, when I assumed total responsibility for my welfare, my destiny, a wake-up call ensued---fast. I began to see how she influenced my steps. She was not just mom, but she was my friend who expected more of me. She wanted me to be free.

I have gained an abundance of appreciation for my mother and her never failing sacrificial love for me.

As an adult I value committed and loving friendships, trust, confidentiality, and community. I am not afraid of being a role model. I can see her shaking her head at me as she said, "Honey, one of these days, you will understand."

I know now where my mother got the faith to assure me that things would be different for me. It is the same Holy Spirit that lived within my mother, Winnie Louise Johnson, and now lives within me.

Today, I proudly say, I am very much like my mother, and I like it that way.

WE NEED TO TALK

I walked in the room
A bit disturbed
At what I saw before me
And before I could think
These words they did leap
From my mouth to address what annoyed me

We need to talk.
That's all I said
And he slowly looked in my direction
I could see the fear written all over his face
As he wondered how to delay this undesired moment of
reflection

We need to talk
Four scary words he just does not like to hear

He looked at me and began to rant
"What's wrong with you today?
Can we do this after the game?
I 'm busy right now,
Besides, we can talk when I am rested

Or when I am in a better mood..."

I just looked at him.
His mouth kept moving, he had more to say

You don't understand that I had a really hard day today
I don't need to deal with anything else right now
Besides, you sure know how to kill a groove
All you want to discuss is business stuff

I rolled my eyes at him. He continued to rant some more.
You used to be fun
We never have fun any more
Because all you want to do is talk, talk, talk
Well I don't want to talk right now

I just shook my head at him. He was on a roll.
He even had the nerve to raise his right foot off the
ground about a half an inch, and stamp it down. He
thinks I missed that quick move, I thought to myself.

He paused as he continued to look at me, trying to judge
whether his theatrics were working

He lowered his voice
Softening his banter
while continuing his position of defense
He then smiled at me and said
Get your hands off your hips girl
I'll fix that "shit"
I know what I'm supposed to do
But I will do it when I get ready to do it

I began counting slowly under my breath
to calm myself down
1, 2, 3....
4, 5.., 6...
I can't believe I am doing this,
7....., 8....,
"Lord help me, please"
9.....
This is it
10

FAMILY

I took a deep breath
And exhaled slowly
I smiled at him sweetly
Then gently but firmly said again
Baby, we need to talk,
And it is happening right now.

WELCOME HOME FLO

The day I bought Flo home, was a funny day. My son, CJ and I were out, and he mentioned to me that they sold cats and dogs at Pets Mart. I had lost my cat Jingles a few months before and had been mentioning getting another cat. I could not believe that they actually sold 4 legged animals at Pets Mart, I had never witnessed it. I knew they sold fish, and pet food and other supplies. I knew they had grooming facilities for your pets, but actually selling dogs and cats...I turned the car in the direction of Pets Mart.

As we walked into the store, right smack in the center aisle was a table where representatives from an animal shelter were showing the animals that were available for adoption. In this cage was a little cat and what appeared to be a ferocious 200 pound dog. She was not even fazed by his presence. (Maybe he wasn't ferocious...I just wondered how much food he ate every day.)

My curiosity caused me to ask questions about her. She was cute, and tiny. They told me she was full grown feline. I was amazed. She practically fit in the palm of my hand...all 6 pounds of her. I had never seen a cat that small that was supposed to be full grown. They told me she was a dwarf cat.

I must have had the sign that says sucker on my forehead that day, because I believed them. They even said if I did not like her I could bring her back, as if she were a pair of shoes that fit too tight.

She was feisty, but sweet and she had one weakness. She became putty in your hands when you rubbed her neck. She would just fall over to enjoy the experience. Liking massages and neck rubs myself, I bonded with her immediately.

We paid for her and promptly named her Flo. I could not wait to show my friends my short haired, tiny, full grown cat with hair that would not shed. She would be a novelty, we had hit the jackpot. They even gave me a crate to take her home in and told me to just drop it back anytime. How is that for service?

So we brought Flo home to Nugget (the dog.) When we walked in the door with her, Nugget (the dog) got excited. She looked at him prancing around and realized that she was going to have to deal with "this dog" that thought she was his new toy (is that not like a man). She had this look on her face that said "another dog."

Then, Flo looked at the "humanoid" sitting in the chair, my husband who looked shocked that we came home and walked with the house with another four legged animal.

As I got ready to explain how it came to be that we left home without a cat and now we had one, Flo jumped into action as if to tell me "I got this." Flo had sized up the situation, decided that this would be an ok place to live and started to "handle the situation." Flo gave Nugget a look that said, I will deal with you later...be cool. Then she sauntered over to my husband, meowed and tried to climb up his leg until he picked her up. You would have sworn she had found her new best friend...what a performance she put on. Flo was incredible.

From then on Flo could do no wrong. I tell you this story as she sits here waiting patiently for me to rub her neck. The feel of the house has a really nice flow since Flo became a part of the family.

YOUR FAMILY

The Position
Among the People
Who give you power
By their presence
Is the Place
You feel most precious
It's so pure.

It's your family
The familiar
It's the fragile
Expectations in the face
Of fantastic
Cherished loving folks

It's your sisters and your brothers
And so many cherished others
Who embrace the bond of tradition
That is so dear
Taking time with one another
Supporting the lives and dreams
of others

Your legacy will be embraced throughout the years

The position
of all familial love
Is profound in what it does
It offers connection
to something greater
It offers power
In the presence
Of the things you hold most precious
It's so pure
It is the family that you love

FAMILY

These are a few songs that remind me of family

- "We Are Family" *by Sister Sledge*
- "Family Reunion" *by the O'Jays*
- "Grandma's Hands" *by Bill Withers*
- "Celebration" *by Kool and the Gang*
- "He Ain't Heavy, He's My Brother" *by The Hollies*
- "Blessed" *by Martina McBride*

What songs remind you of family?

FRIENDS

CONVERSATION WITH MY GIRLFRIEND

Sit down girlfriend

I need to talk to you

I understand what you are going through

You see I have been there before

And I have had to endure

Pain from the bruises inflicted on me

By others and myself

But you need to know that

Given a little bit of time

You will find that

Things will get better

The scars you now display

Will one day disappear

And no one will see them or know about them

Unless you find you cannot let go of them

Let go my sister,

So the healing can begin.

The past is the past

That you cannot change

Embrace what you have learned

Have faith in yourself

Believe that you are worthy

To be the person you want to be
Speak it
Act on it
Become it
It is yours if you want it
Knowing there will be sacrifices you will have to make
Again,
But this time
You are in control
As you begin your today
Which will lead to your tomorrow
And please know
As someone who only sees the good in you
And wants the best for you
And will support you as long as I have breath in this
body
I am your girlfriend
My dear sister-friend
And I will be standing near always
As you do for me
Girlfriend

FROM MY HEAD TO MY TOES

I cannot believe
How fast my hair grows
Not on my head
Not under my arms
Not even the hair that I shave from my legs
I just cannot believe
How fast this hair grows

I am aware that hair grows
From my head to my toes
But this hair is causing
So many woes

This hair seems to grow
So long over night
On the areas that lie
Right under my nose

By now you should know
Just where this hair grows
It just grows and it grows
Causing me so many woes

It's on my chinny-chin-chin

My chinny, chin-chin

I thought this only happened to men

HE CAN BARK

Nugget is the four legged
tail wagging
pleasure causing animal in our house
who allows us to love him, feed him
walk him
play with him
and enjoy him every day.
He's especially playful and outgoing.
All the neighbors know him
because he makes it a point to
greet them every chance he gets,
He loves to share his love.

For months I didn't think he could bark
or was interested in barking.
Even when he would get a chance to play with a few of
his playmates in the neighborhood,
he never barked.
Then one night I let him out to run
and heard this strange sounding noise outside my door

It was the barking of a dog I had never heard before

FRIENDS

It wasn't Riley or Daisy or the yippie yappie dog with the
high pitched bark that growls at everything in the
neighborhood that moves.

I looked outside
and to my surprise
I saw that Nugget had found his voice.
He ran around barking with authority
while chasing deer out of the yard to protect the
boundaries of his family
his tail began wagging happily back and forth
knowing he had found his calling
his purpose,
he circled the yard
barking with content,
announcing to all who could see or hear
That he, Nugget, man's best friend
Was and continues to be protector of the family

Yes, Nugget can bark.

I CAN'T SEEM TO GET MYSELF TOGETHER

I could not seem to get myself together
because I did not know where I was going
Anymore

The path I planned had gone asunder
As I watched all that I had lived for
Be destroyed

I tried mightily to fight
The steady wave of parasites
pushing my hopes far from sight
blocking my view of any light

Then fear raised its vicious head to take the final bite as I
was falling apart
feeling broken
I was so scared

Even though I could not visualize
What life would offer
I knew then that I had to get myself together

No longer willing to watch the dreams fade
That once directed my life
I grasped on to hope
Preceded by miracles revealed through prayer

I got up, slowly
Then I looked around
To see what called my name
As I was curious about experiencing
A new and different vein

I soon began to change

I turned to see a new direction
I began moving uninhibited
Although curious thoughts made me question
Whether I could survive the fight

I asked myself
What am I supposed to give
That will express all the years
What am I supposed to leave
That will serve another who is in need

I told myself to
"Get a grip on your situation
do not sacrifice the ride
Embrace the joy of your imperfection"

Suddenly, I realized that I
As myself
Am as together as I will ever be
As long as I accept the changes
Deep inside of me

I COULD NOT SLEEP

I could not sleep, so many thoughts were running through my mind. I also did not think you would appreciate me calling you so early in the morning, so I thought I would share some of my thoughts with you by e-mail.

It is 5 am and the world outside is really coming alive. As I sit in the midst of it, I wonder what am I to do with all of this that God has blessed me with. I understand that having life and hope embodies everything.

I'm sitting outside at nature's door and viewing the miraculous beauty that only God can create. The trees before me stand tall and beautiful. They are full of thriving lushness. Each leaf is a beautiful work of art. Not only is it a work of art but a functional part of things that add to man's life.

We know the color green because of the leaves. We also recognize that its life cycle can take this little leaf through many stages...much like man. From green to yellow to brown, or maybe green to warm autumn tones of red, and orange, then to brown.

While they are vibrant they provide beauty for us to view, shade for us to stand under, music to our ears when the wind blows through and around them. It also provides privacy from others looking in our direction. It serves as a place to play as we remember our childhood games, lean against for support as we reminisce and even a place to etch our permanent love and devotion to that one who captured our heart when we were young. I can see how a little tiny seedling becomes a strapping well planted tree standing firm in its spot of the world. It provides shelter for birds and other life forms. The tree even provides food, which is vital for all living beings.

Yes, maybe we view a tree as a simple life form, but its makeup is very complex...much like me.

Have a wonderful day,
Regina

I THOUGHT I WAS WALKING ALONE.

I thought I was walking alone.
The storm that was brewing in my life was coming to a
head
I was nervous, a bit fearful, and confused.

Then all of a sudden I noticed that there was a band of
women around me.
They were supporting me to do whatever I thought was
right.
They passed no judgment, they made no suggestions.
They just supported me so that I could stand tall.

My vulnerabilities came through and there they were,
circling around me
To keep me safe, so I could stand strong.
As I shed my tears of pain, they wiped my eyes and said
We are here so that you can do what you must do,

I know what I must do is stand strong, and be strong.
How did I ever think that I thought I was alone?
I am never alone, because I have my circle of friends,
Surrounding me, so that I can stand strong.

INGRID

I remember lying in my bed and looking in the dark, and not being able to see a thing. All I could hear was the roaring of the Pacific Ocean which was literally within 150 yards of the cottage where my dear friend Ingrid and I were staying. It belonged to her mother and Ingrid had invited me to join her so we could enjoy the solitude and beauty of nature at its finest.

This time spent together turned out to be the foundation of our friendship as girlfriends.

Normally, when I am in a different environment and it is extremely dark with no nightlight I tend to feel on the scary side. I was ok because I had my friend, Ingrid in the same space with me and she was comfortable in this place that was familiar to her. I was able to feel settled in the dark surroundings knowing that the "boogie man" would not show up.

As we both lay in our separate twin bunk beds, we talked. We were not the best of friends before that time. We were two women, over 10 years apart in age who somehow connected with one another with no effort.

We met at "Bankprint Company" where we were hired as outside sales people for them. I started about two weeks before Ingrid and as soon as she was hired many of the people we worked with began to get our names mixed up. They would call me Ingrid and call her Regina. It became a joke between the two of us, because we looked nothing alike. There were absolutely no physical similarities between us. I am tall, she is about 4 inches shorter, I am black, she is white, I have (had) black hair, she has this stunning strawberry blonde hair and the list of differences goes on and on.

Our work experience was the beginning of our friendship. It was a gift we received through circumstance. It led to over 30 years of true friendship that time or distance has not been able to dissolve.

As we lay chatting, our idle banter eased into something more substantial and real. Protected by the dark we were safe enough to let all barriers down and share secrets that we had not spoken to many, if any people before that day. They were the types of secrets that women sometimes live and die with. They were secrets that many times shape women for all the days before them.

These secrets included hurt, embarrassment, betrayal and even regret. These were secrets that would normally remain unspoken. Our shared secrets that made us both cry and laugh, and now remain a memory for just for the two of us.

As I lay there in the dark listening, I realized the strength of this amazing woman. I could not see her but I felt every word she spoke as if it were my experience. Her history which was her soul she freely shared with me. This in turn allowed me to let go myself of my private trials knowing that I would not be harmed. I was safe, she was safe and we together shared pieces of our lives that would forever bind us together.

Life has thrown both of us many challenges and many happy moments as well. Through the years we have seen each other through marriage, divorce, children, death, life changes, body changes, sickness and so much more. We have had some disagreements. There were times we made unspoken but conscious decisions not to discuss certain things because we were so passionate about our difference of opinions.

Time has allowed both of us to mellow out. Today, we don't have any taboo subjects and we don't care or worry if the other feels differently about something that might be said. In spite of the difference in age, background, race, experiences and interest we have always liked each other, respected each other, and been able to laugh at each other --even the tough moments where we have had to admit and say, "If I had just listened to what you were telling me, things might have been different." They were not, but we had each other to lean on to get us through our "situations."

We both have a lot of living to do, and it is good to know that we will always have each other.

I will forever remember that moment where Ingrid and I were comfortable enough to let down all the walls of protection that normally keep us "safe," as we talked until the wee hours in the morning in that dark cottage, until there was no more to say. Then quiet ensued as we were rocked to sleep by the sound of the ocean waves which were roaring loudly. So like the ocean that goes on and on but is always there, our friendship has been as steady and constant.

INSPIRED BY MY FRIENDSHIP WITH YOU

I am inspired by the kindness I receive

From the warm and loving woman you are to me.

I am humbled by the friendship

It warms my soul,

The priceless gift you give to me helps me to be bold.

You walk ahead

I follow you

I honor you

I mimic you

I learn from you

I see you through the things that one day I will do.

But most of all I thank God for you

Who allows me to see what a real woman can do.

NUGGET AND FLO

Having animals is a treat in life. They bring so much joy to a household. Having pets has offered another insight to life for me. I have seen how love grows from someone who is very different than me, as I watched the relationship/friendship between Nugget and Flo materialize before my eyes. It really shows me that love is something that is natural, and easily occurs, if I have a willing heart.

Nugget is my dog and he is a very happy dog. So much so, he has not yet met anyone or anything (of the two legged species) that he thinks does not adore him. Nugget is always willing to share his love, whether I want it or not. He charges at friends as well as strangers, with enthusiasm, his tail wagging back and forth. I always have to explain he is still really a puppy. My neighbor said for me to expect him to be this boisterous for another two years.

Nugget is such a popular dog, all the neighbors know him, even though I do not know all the neighbors. I will be out walking him, and people walking by will say, "hi Nugget." Then will ask me "are you Nugget's mom." I want to ask them sometimes, "Where exactly did you meet Nugget?" Instead I just smile because I realize that Nugget is far more popular than I will ever be.

Then there is Flo, my beautiful distinctive looking she-cat. Large splashes of gray fur against a snow white fur background. She has an aristocratic and very elegant way about her. When she enters a room, she pauses so-- to make sure that you are aware that she has decided to share a few moments of her precious time with you. Once you acknowledge her, she will politely meow you. This means you are dismissed, and can go back to whatever you were doing. Meow.

Every morning at 5:30, she pounces on the bed to let me know that she would like me to get up and open the window shade. Once I do, she glides onto my grandmother's cedar chest, which provides me a place to sit, read and store memories while looking out of the window. This chest is old but it is full of love and has followed me around for almost 40 years of my life.

Flo likes to sit and gaze out of the window. Most often, it is still dark, but I noticed, human being that I am, that she likes to watch the new day begin. She stretches and she lies down and acts as if she is in seventh heaven. I believe it must set the tone for her day. Around 6:15, Nugget will come in from wherever he hangs out while everyone sleeps and jumps on the chest and sits with her. Side by side they watch the world come to light. Sometimes I wonder if they see what I see or hear the birds singing as I do. All I know is that together gazing out of the window, the three of us are content in the moment.

Sometimes I watch them and it makes me smile because I think about the fact that dogs and cats are really not supposed to care for each other. I am not sure where that fallacy came from because that is not the case in this house. Nugget and Flo have deep affection for each other. They fight with each other, they chase each other around the house, they worry about each other when one is uncomfortable, they protect each other, and they even snuggle and lick each other in the face, often in view of anyone around.

And we call them animals.

MY RANDOM THOUGHTS ABOUT A GOOD SMELLING MAN

From my perspective, there is nothing quite as nice as a man who smells good.

A good smelling man will gives me something to smile about, because he leaves me with a positive impression. A lingering thought. A welcoming reminder. For a moment he has sparked one of my senses and I feel alive.

When I say this I am not necessarily speaking of a man I am in a relationship with or even have any interest in...it can be any good smelling man. As I go about my day, and perhaps have a conversation with someone of the opposite sex, I, like anyone else, usually take in a lot of information. When my sense of smell is pleasantly engaged, it usually makes the interaction more memorable.

When I am with a man who smells good the first thing I think is, "have mercy." Nothing sexual is intended in this thought process, but his just being there even for a moment has lifted my spirit and probably made me smile. That is worth a lot in this woman's day. It's one of those things I would mention to another woman whom I am friendly with.

Whenever I encounter HIM, and I get a whiff of Citrus notes combined with sandalwood... the aroma just sends me to the moon and I smile all the way back.

Yes, from my perspective, there is nothing quite as nice as a good smelling man.

THE UTILITY OF THE THONG

I went to my lingerie drawer and decided to grab a pair of panties from the back. Out came the thong. My goodness I had not worn a thong in years, in fact I thought I had disposed of all of them. I had to sit down and smile because I remember the conversation I had with my mother over 30 years ago, about how impractical she thought thongs were.

Being in my early 20's I just thought they were sexy, because that was what all the women were buying because that was what the fashion industry was selling as sizzling hot for women who wanted to feel and be sexy.

Count me in, I was one of them.

And the sexiness was not for a man, it was more for me. I saw no lines when I wore my skin tight jeans that we all wore. In fact the tighter the jeans the better, and panty lines were a no-no.

My mother asked me a simple question, "Why would you want a piece of fabric stuck in the crack of your ass all day long?" I looked at her and said, "really mommy."

Then she went on to say "It seems as if it would be uncomfortable. They need to fit relatively tight in order to feel snug, and if they don't fit well, that would be even worse. It also seems there may be more of a chance they would soil easier..." although she did not use that terminology.

I just laughed at her, and told her she was old fashioned. Over the next few days, I started paying attention to how my thong fit. Did it rub, did it irritate, was I always aware of the fact that I had them on, which fabric felt better on my skin all day? Cotton, silk, lace, silky polyester...it really did not matter, because now I was aware that I did feel the thong all day in the crack of my ass.

As I thought this all out, I acknowledged that I was not involved with anyone so I did not really need to wear them to look sexy...no one was going to see them. Well, maybe other women while I was changing clothes in a locker room at the gym, or some of my friends when we were out shopping and trying on clothes.

I soon decided I could wear my bikini underwear, and still feel sexy for myself. I found that I did not have the slight annoyance that my mother made me think of in how that thong really felt.

So today, thirty plus years after that conversation, I decided to once again put on a pair of thongs. And yes, they do fit. But just like my mother said, I can feel them in the crack of my ass, still. It's not terribly uncomfortable, but I am aware of it. Now, that I am single again, much like before, there will be no one to see them who would think that they are sexy. These days I go to the gym usually fully dressed and ready to work-out, my cat and dog couldn't care less about me wearing clothes. The only thing they think about is doing a trick for a pat and a rub or a snack.

So, my friend, I sit here smiling, wearing my thong that I can feel in the crack of my ass, wanting to know, did you ever think about thongs like this, or is it just me...?

WHO IS THAT MAN I MARRIED?

Every now and then, I like to sit, relax and enjoy a really nice glass of wine. I prefer red wine, usually a cabernet or a merlot. To satisfy my taste buds for both varieties of grapes used for the wine, I will often opt for a bordeaux. With my glass of wine, I imagine myself in France, in a countryside setting. I am sitting on a blanket, under a tall shade tree, taking in the beautiful and fragrant field of lavender which surrounds me in every direction. My picnic basket is filled with warm crusty bread, tasty cheeses and fresh fruit and of course the bottle of wine.

Usually I'm by myself because I enjoy the solitude. Sometimes I'm with friends and we sit enjoying the moment chatting while enjoying the moment. A few times I would envision this scene with my husband, now my ex. The adjustment I had with him in my dream is we each had to have our own bottle of wine because he only likes a sweet white wine. We don't even enjoy the same wine. Oh well.

Our differences in the wines we liked parallels the differences we had when it came to relating to each other. We did not like enough of the same things that were important to each of us. Good wine gets better with age. Bad wine, try as you might, cannot be improved and still call it wine.

The thought I am about to share is one I had while married. It holds true in spite of the outcome between my ex and myself.

I remember laughing at a picture of an older man and a woman sitting at a table seemingly enjoying themselves as they each sipped on a glass of wine. The essence of the message that accompanied the picture was:

The woman closes her eyes and states "I don't know what I would do without you, some days I just could not make it if I did not have you." She wasn't talking to her partner; she was talking to the wine.

I have to admit that there have been days when I have felt that I am talking to a glass of wine for sanity's sake. These are the days when I think that my husband has totally lost his mind. Sometimes, it takes every bit of strength that I have to remain halfway calm so that we can get to the issue at heart.

Marriage and relationships are not easy. The courtship is easy, because everyone is usually on fairly good behavior. Once a commitment is made and comfort sets into the relationship, surprise elements in personality and behavior may emerge. There probably will be difficult times.

To stay engaged and in love takes more than talking to the glass of wine. We should always be sincere in our communication with our partner. If we can be sweet because of a glass of wine we must be as sweet without a glass of wine. We may have to constantly ask ourselves the question posed at the beginning, "Who Is That Man I Married?" You can only answer honestly after you take time to remember the "Why." Why did you want and choose to marry him? The reference to the wine is so powerful. Marriage takes constant work and nurturing each and every day. Remember the wine.

FRIENDS

Music makes me feel good. Spending time with friends also makes me feel good.

Here are a few songs that remind me of friends.

- "You've Got a Friend" *by James Taylor*
- "Best Friend" *by Brandy*
- "Lean On Me" *by Bill Withers*
- "You've Got A Friend In Me" *by Randy Newman*
- "Thank-you For Being a Friend *by Andrew Gold*
- "I'll Be There For You" *by The Rembrandts*
- "With A Little Help From My Friends" *by John Lennon and Paul McCartney*

What songs would you have on your list?

DESIRE

A LOVER IN MY MIDST

What I wouldn't give today
To have a really good lover in my home to play
I don't want him to stay for too long
Just long enough for the two of us to sing that song

I'm willing to let him rock my little world
While I will certainly assist the mood as it unfurls
With the understanding that he can only stay
For a little while today

I just fancy having a remembrance of the thrill
Of romancing once again until
My body says it's time to chill
Until the next time that I will
Get that feeling I sometimes miss
When there is not a lover in my midst

I WAS

I was cute,
I was young
I was alive and ready for anything the world presented
before me, as mine.

Even when it came to affection or adoration from men.
I thought they had good taste because I was a princess.
My father had told me this so many times and again.

I did not understand the pain another woman would feel
because eyes that were once captivated by her
now focused on me.
All I could see was how exciting this bit of appreciation
for me
bore tremendous exhilaration for me.

I was young,
I was cute,
I was alive but in many ways
I was dumb
not to understand the realities of what pain a woman
feels when her lover forgets

that he is her love,
and begins to cast his affections towards another without
as much as a blink of an eye.

When a woman is in love
And her love suddenly finds reasons to criticize her ways,
her looks,
her demeanor and her eyes
as if she does not see that he
is no longer focused on her
because he had his attention directed on someone who
was perhaps like me.
The fault finding was his excuse.
I now know it was a lie.

I'm a grown ass woman now,
But I do remember that once upon a time I was dumb
And did some really dumb things, for which I am sorry
And for which I have had to bear the responsibility that
my selfish actions may have hurt an innocent woman
who was already hurting
because she had feelings, very much like mine...

But at the time I was cute,
Yes, I was young and I was very much alive,

and I was ready for anything the world presented to me as mine.

I WISH I HAD A MAN

I wish I had a man
Who wanted to hold me close
Squeeze me so
Then let me go as he backed up just a bit
And took his hand
And so gently lifted my chin so my eyes could look into
his
And I would see his smile as he looked at me
Then he would take his index finger and gently trace the
outside of my face
As I continued to look at him.
His finger would stop as he gently caressed the back of
my neck
He would move in closer to me
Then with his face so near to mine,
He would bend even closer to me, so smoothly, and kiss
me, sweetly.
Wow, yes I do wish I had a man who would let me know
By the way he stops dead in his tracks, as I walk by
the look on his face lets me know that I am his only
pleasure for the moment
as he looks at me
And that look that I see says he loves only me

Because of this he knows and I know that I would forever
be his.
If I had this man, I would love this man.
I would forever care for this man,
I would treat him like the man
I would honor him as a man
Who loves me like no other man can
Yes, one day, I will have a man like the man that today I
wish I had.

LAMENT TO LOVE

It's been a long time since I have made love
Because for a long time I didn't have real love
Because I spent a long time with the wrong love
Who turned out not to be my true love
Boohoo, Boohoo, I'm sad Boohoo

My friends told me not to jump into love
But I thought I could manage "this being in love"
Indeed, it's been surreal love
Because I'm not sure who he really loves
So sad, Boohoo, I'm Blue, Boohoo

I know that it wasn't me love
Because he didn't show he cared for me with love
He said if I wanted him to love
I would have to give up me for love
I'm Blue, Boohoo, I'm sad, Boohoo

I gave up me for a while to see if love
Could be the way I needed love
For years I waited to receive his love
But never experienced unrestricted love
So Blue, Boohoo, So Blue, Boohoo

DESIRE

I yearned for him to call me love
I cried many tears for this love
There was much pain instead of love
I closed my eyes and imagined love
I was so blue, so sad and blue

He said that he could not feel the love
And I should settle for the appearance of love
He thought that would allow him to chase around for
love
In others beds and call it love
Hell no, I'm through, although, I'm Blue

I only wanted him to be nice and love
The promise he made to me in love
So many years ago when love
Was a fantasy I dreamed I would love
I'm through, oh yes this time I'm through

It has been a long time since I have made love
Because I chose the wrong man to love
But I have once again found my real true love
And it is me my forever love
This time, I'm through, I'm happy, too.

WHEN YOU MAKE LOVE

When you make love,
It is very different than having sex.
Both feel good,
But the term "a roll in the hay" is an uncommitted,
reality of the act
You get what you get.
No real expectations, just hope that it is worth your time.

Making love is very different.
It can take eroticism to another level as
two people who are present for each other
commit the mind, the soul and the body and
the desire for the other one who is within their reach
this allows them to become one

Sometimes all of us like a roll in the hay.
It requires no commitment, no caring, just the self-
seeking pleasure you can get.
The problem is after the roll in the hay,
Someone is usually left feeling like an unappreciated,
unneeded piece of meat.
Tasty, but not fulfilling.

DESIRE

When you make love,
you are aware of the heart that lies close to you,
the warmth of the tender touch caressing your body,
and your touch feeling all of him...or her

When you make love your head is full of them
and you instinctively want to give them all you have
When you make love

When you make love
as your lips brush theirs
and their lips slightly part to allow your tongue to be that
lollipop in their mouth
and the juiciness is shared between the two of you
And yes it is tasty and it is sweet
And it also lingers long after you have made love

When you make love
She will yearn for the feel of your man-ness as it enters
her garden of treasures that are sacred and saved only to
be enjoyed by you.
When you make love

You plant the seed

She nurtures the seed

And something more beautiful is born.

When you make love

it feels good,

much like sex

except sex, just sex

will never feel all the things you will feel

When you make love

DESIRE

There are those individuals that seem to make us loose our minds when they are near ...

- "Let's Get It On" *by Marvin Gaye*
- "Do Ya Think I'm Sexy" *by Rod Stewart*
- "I'll Make Love To You" *by Boyz To Men*
- "Physical" *by Olivia Newton-John*
- "Hot Stuff" *by Donna Summer*
- "Natural Woman" *by Aretha Franklin*
- "Son Of A Preacher Man" *by Dusty Springfield*

Did I leave a song out that should be part of the above list?

BONUS GIFT

A bonus gift **Reflections of Love**, will allow you to continue the reflections started with
Sometimes He Buys Me Grapes.

For your free copy go to
http://www.sometimeshebuysmegrapes.com/ROLbook

Family * Friends * Desire

Love * The Break-Up

Moving On * Back To Me

LOVE

A MAN'S FIRST LOVE... "JALOPY"

The WIKIPEDIA definition for Jalopy is a decrepit car, often old and in a barely functional state. It is also referred to as a clunker or hooptie.

The first love affair many men had in their lives was with a car, better known as "jalopy." In conversations with men about their infatuation with their unforgettable first car, it becomes apparent that this was an awesome love affair for most of them. I cannot even imagine the number of men that have been caught, in the trap of love, with a vehicle whose tires treaded its way into their hearts.

From my lifetime of observing this phenomenon I can boldly state that it does not even have to be a new car. In fact I will even go as far to say that it is even a rite of passage for some men to gain ownership of a broken down, bent up piece of metal that one can hear coming in your direction two blocks away. The only thing that men care about is that this car runs because they can see its true potential. "Jalopy" is fondly remembered as a diamond in the rough...a real treasure.

In fact I believe that men see a sleek, sexy macho car, when in fact they may actually own something everyone else views as a jalopy. I have seen guys looking at their four-wheeled contraptions, and seemingly go into a trance as if they were star struck just thinking about "Jalopy."

There is not a detail they cannot remember. They know the color, make, year, what kind of gas "Jalopy" needs, what size tires and even the interior seat colors.

The funny thing is that most of the jalopies are given female names. It is not unusual to hear a guy talking about Norma, Betty or Shanaynay in such an affectionate way, only to realize they are talking about a "jalopy." They love "her" so much they will sometimes buy car jewelry or adornments to dangle on or near the dashboard, proudly. I've seen everything from fuzzy dice to mini wind chimes hanging off the rear view mirror. What a sight to behold.

When you factor the freedom and experience that a man experienced when Jalopy came on the scene, one realizes that a new man was born.

I was talking to Michael, a friend I have known forever. I consider Michael a man of few words...a deep thinker. When I asked him about his jalopy he gave me a long dissertation about his car. The smile on his face showed pleasure and his choice of words were full of unrequited love.

I sat with a stoic look on my face as Michael went on and on talking about his jalopy that he named Betsy. When he started talking about her unique aroma and how it made him feel as he sat snug in the driver's seat behind the furry steering wheel, I burst out in laughter. I had heard enough about Betsy, jalopy or whatever he wanted to call his clunker of a first love.

One thing for sure, a conversation about Jalopy will definitely be an interesting time remembering special times from "back in the day."

By the way, do you remember how much gas was then?

The

very

scent

of

him

is

unforgettable!!!

I START EACH DAY

I start my day with my creator who I am an image of
I start my day with him
I start my day with her

The spirit of the creator is so strong
Which allows me to cast aside my doubts
as I march to fulfill the path that I must tell the world
about

Wearing armor as my gear
I step beyond my fear
Following the laws of love
My creator is always near

Detours try to blind
me from my view,
my mission,
my goal...
and most of all,
my time,
it tries to rob me blind

More time with my creator puts me on my path once
more

That is why each and every day
I choose to start my day
With my maker, my creator, my source of strength
There is none greater

I am grateful that I can say
I am unique in every way
Made in the image of the one
Who lovingly oversees my day
Until the day is done

And so it is

LIFE IS SO VERY SHORT

Life is so very short. I wish that I myself had never wasted one moment of my precious time being mad, negative or feeling unfulfilled. I wish that I had done everything I possibly could to bring joy to anyone I came into contact with. I wish that I could have stopped long enough to help someone who needed my assistance. But most of all I wish that I could have loved those close to me much better than I have.

Life allows us to make better choices and, with age, a more enlightened person comes forth, so as I acknowledge that, even though I am regretful about all that I have not done up to this point, I am committed to make each and every day in front of me, much better than the day before.

Will You?

I send you love.

MEMORIES ARE FOREVER

There is something remarkable about the mind. It stores the memories of your past. This allows you to feel comfort and love at the strangest times.

I remember when my uncle was suffering from dementia and he could not remember who he was talking to or what happened yesterday. He could surprisingly recall pleasant memories that took place over fifty years ago.

You have memories that will be with you forever, because memories are forever.

SPIRIT OF VALOR

I was sitting in church one Sunday, and the men's chorus was singing, "We Are the Mighty Men of Valor." As they sang, my spirit was filled with appreciation and gratefulness. Sitting next to my close friends, Gwen and Phil, as I did every Sunday, my eyes started to burn as the emotion of what I was hearing registered in my heart. Gwen, noticing the tears, handed me a tissue to wipe my eyes.

My husband and I were separated at the time. He was living on the East Coast and I was living on the West Coast. My son was living with me. I was a working mother juggling everything alone and determined to make it work. At times I felt overwhelmed, sad and confused as I tried to figure out why the relationship between my husband and me had become so strained. It was difficult for us to hold a pleasant conversation, and the only thing we seemed to have in common at this point was the love we both had for our son.

It seemed so weird to be in this place because at one time I considered him to be more than just my husband, he was my best friend. "Was" can be such a sad word.

As I looked in the choir stand, and then around at the congregation, a great peace and realization came over me. I knew I was in a safe and caring place. Most of the men, women and children here felt like family, although some were more distant than others as is always the case in a community of people. I knew, beyond a shadow of a doubt that if I needed anything, support wise, there were people all around who had love for my family and they would be there for me, my son and my husband. I had seen it over and over when a family or individual was "going through the storm" people in this community stepped in to offer a bit of assurance to ease the pain when it was fresh and at its worst--the women making sure a woman had a friend to talk to and the men making sure they could assist in the heavy lifting of things...usually handling it amongst themselves so they could at least put a band-aid on what needed fixing.

Yes, we had many eyes looking out for us. From time to time I would notice one of the men would pull my son aside for "man talk." I remember one day we got to church and CJ was not happy about the suit I made him wear. John saw CJ's displeasure with mommy, bent down to his level, talked to him for a moment, made some adjustments that only work when done by a man for a younger man, then in a flash, everything was good.

His godfather stepped in even more to spend time with his godson, never missing a game and making sure that he knew he was loved and supported. CJ never had to feel the lack of a man's presence who loved him as his own.

So, with my tear stained face and cherry red eyes, I felt blessed as the beautiful tenor and bass voices sang boldly and confidently "We are the mighty, mighty men of valor..."

These men were indeed warriors who had a history of showing up with courage, gallantry, spirit and a loving heart. Yes, these mighty men of valor embraced the true spirit of valor.

MY MAN

I have been looking for my man,
Have you seen him?
You will know that IT IS HE,
WHEN YOU SEE him
There will be a twinkle in his eyes
Whenever I walk by
Because this man knows for sure that
He is my man

I may not notice him at first
But that's ok
Because my man knows that someday
He will have his way,
He will understand that it takes time
To secure love that is sublime
Because this man will know that he is mine
Yes, he is my man

One day I'll turn around and see him there
In all his strength, with all his love, and all his care
He will offer me his hand
Which I will not reprimand

I will nurture I will honor
All he provides, protects and honors
Because he is my man, my one true man

So if you see me looking for my man
And you know that it is my man
You can whisper in my ear
To make sure I really hear
That before me is the gift that I do seek
And he has claimed me as the present he will reap
As a reward for understanding
That this amazing man beside me
Is more than just a man
He's my man

My only man
My loving man
My faithful man
To whom I give my heart
He has my heart
Yes, my man

STANDING IN THE FIRE

As I stand here in the fire
I realize that I am not alone
I am shielded with the power
From my Father up above

His arms will keep me standing
though I am feeling weak
I guess things needed rearranging
So I could get past this defeat

My faith sometimes gets shaky
but its presence never leaves
Because I know that I will conquer
any burning flames the fire will leave

There is a spirit that surrounds me
it gives me hope and joy and more
Yes, I am shielded with the power
From my Father up above

REGINA GALE

THANK-YOU LORD

My eyes opened this morning, and I looked around
to see what I could see,
and all was sound
I smiled and knew that I'd been favored, yes amen
I cried out Thank-you Lord for watching over me again

I have been blessed another day
and I hope that I can say
that I can bless another person
along the way

Each day becomes more pivotal as
I think often about the miracles of my life

All that l can really say,
as I get started on my way is
THANK YOU LORD
for loving me each day

YOUR TIME

You need to hear me say this one more time
what I need from you is quality time
I understand you are busy, and that's all fine
But when you're with me,
I feel that time should be mine

I am as important to you
as anything else should ever be
Although I am your biggest fan,
I am not here to serve
Your every beck and call
especially when it seems
you have little time for me at all

I am your mate
Your partner in life,
I want to protect the wall
that encompasses us all
But the one caveat that I do expect
is that the people in this home be treated with respect

I understand that it takes time to reach the goals
that you have set

But your family is the reason those goals were even set
So if your climb still includes those who are feeling left
behind
to make us happy all we ask from you is a little bit of
your time

When I am with you
I feel secure in the love that you vowed to protect

That is what gives me strength as I mend the worries of
the day
while holding down the fort when you are away

I don't mean to nag
I am not saying that you don't care
But I need more of you
Than you currently share

Let us lay it all on the line
so we can survive the fate of time
one day you and I will be old
but still want to be together here as one
To do so we must not take for granted

what we have right here, right now

LOVE

All I am trying to say is
When you and I are together
let's make it quality time.
With this as our priority we will never fail
good times, bad times, whatever we will prevail

I love you and I need you
I am grateful for our moments
we are able to share without any fuss
knowing nothing is promised
so let's not throw any time that could be our time away

So when you are really busy
Please know you are on my mind
And remember all I need from you my love,
is a little quality time

* LOVE*

Love is such an honest emotion. When you feel love and have love, everything is beautiful. Here are some songs about love.

- "Love Will Keep Us Together" *by Captain & Tennille*
- "All You Need Is Love" *by The Beatles*
- "I Just Called To Say I Love You" *by Stevie Wonder*
- "Greatest Love of All" *by Whitney Houston*
- "Endless Love" *by Diana Ross & Lionel Richie*

Add your favorites to this list.

THE BREAK UP

ANOTHER DAY

I don't have the heart to stay
And do this thing another day
My soul is gone
And I am barely holding on
To a life where I feel that I no longer belong

I didn't plan on this transition
I didn't have a choice after recognition
That my foundation had been rocked and it was gone
I tried hard but I was barely holding on

I was too afraid to see what was before me
I did not want to see that we no longer were a we
I thought my strength
Would fix the length of divide
That had grown disproportionately wide over time

I will not let fear
Keep me here
Another year
Where I stand alone
Even when you are oh so near

Yes, your feelings allowed you to act without regard
To a love that was yours but you did not guard
No need to explain
You made it very plain
Your actions were heard
I got the word
It is what you preferred

And now I no longer have the heart to stay with you
Another day.

GOOD-BYE

Baby, you have got to go
You can't stay with me no more
I'm tired of your lies
And you don't even try
To build the life you promised me
That day you fell down on your knees
And pledged your love to me

It broke my heart to find you
Tipping around,
Playing the clown.
So-o-o
Touch down,
Tore down,
Love down,
You're down
You have caused my love for you to shut down

You said you would never be
Neglectful to me,
The vows that we shared
You treated as dead

THE BREAK UP

You wanted respect
You threw that away
Making decisions as if
You could throw your family away
So it seemed, you weren't part of our scene
You did your own thing
Then left us again

Big man
No plan
Children raised by other men
Money, I make it
Now you want to take it
Get your ass out my house
Because you are acting just like a louse
Running games on me
Like I'm a stranger to thee
Get your ass out the door
You are not welcome here anymore

So-o-o,
Like I said before
Touch down,
Tore down,

Love down,

You're down

You have caused my love for you to shut down

GOOD-BYE -PART TWO

Are you back again?

You have got to go

You can't stay with me any more

Yes, I am sad

But I am no longer mad

About the years

Or all the tears

You have a need

To be carefree

So I say go

I want you to soar

Evermore

My love for you

Has always been true

But I need more

Than you want to give

I have a life I want to live

So this is good-bye

All actions comply
You made a choice
And I found my voice

For the very last time
The consequential outcome is
Touch down,
Tore down,
Love down,
You're down
My love for you is shut down

FORSAKING ALL OTHERS

Forsaking all others forever
Was the promise we made at the start
Of the journey we began together
To protect till death do us part

I now find that my journey is lonely
Since you chose a road that was not part of our plan
But I have faith that my path will show me
New graces as I start again

Forsaking all others forever
Was more precious than you will ever know
My fork in the road now allows me
Good direction with purpose and goals

Forsaking all others for ever
Was the promise we made from the start
Forsaking all others forever
Meant loving till death do us part,
It meant, loving till death do us part

I HAVE BEEN TO HELL...AND I WORE IT WELL

My grown, divorced nephew asked me a question I did not know if I could answer...at least not in a way that would make any sense to him. He asked, "Why would you stay with my uncle, for all these years, if he was so bad?"

At first all I could say is, "I just did."

How do I explain to a man, that as a woman, the tendency to nurture the man I love is strong. Even when things were bad, the little bit of good I saw in my man, made me want to stay and try to fix it. I just could not give up.

I found myself trying to recreate those good memories. I wanted to relive that joy from the past and place it in my present. It just didn't work for me, or us.

According to "My Man For Life List" I knew beyond a doubt that he should have been my perfect mate. There was a side of him I loved, and will always love. But that side of him never seemed to stay too long, no matter how hard I kept trying to pull him closer to me. We both liked our space, but he needed more space. The closeness required to make our marriage work was too close for comfort for him.

I admit, he was caring, smart and fun to be with. He still **is** all those things, but that was not enough for me. He just was not, is not nor has he ever been responsible enough for me.

The burden and responsibility I had to carry alone much of the time was even heavier due to the lack of respectability when it came down to the word "we," and it was killing me.

I was drained of everything I had, and I had nothing left to give him. He was way overdrawn and I saw no attempt or concern to make a deposit into my or our lives...beyond his terms, his time, his choice, as if I had no voice and I shouldn't even care. But I did, and I do.

It took me a long time to admit to myself that I was fighting for something I could not win. If it was not a win-win situation, then we both were going to be losers. There is no middle when it comes to love.

I needed him to be honest with me.

I needed him to do the things he said he would do.

I needed to know that he would do his best to protect and try to provide for me, or sometimes just hold me, and tell me that what we had was precious and worth any bit of sacrifice that either of us would make, because we would do it together.

I needed to trust him.

I needed that, I craved that...I didn't have that. I knew I would never have it with him.

I just got tired of making hell look so good.

LOVE IS NOT ABOUT A FEELING

My ex had the nerve to tell me once that he did not "feel" love for me; therefore he could not, did not and would not say I love you, to me.

I was rendered speechless by his proclamation. I just shook my head in amazement as I wondered how anyone as old as he, could not understand that love is not about a feeling. Love is about commitment.

It was my understanding that we both believed the definition of love as truth, as it is found in the bible.

1 Corinthians 13: 4-8
Love is patient

Love is kind

It does not envy

It does not boast

It is not proud

It does not dishonor others

It is not self-seeking

It is not easily angered

It keeps no record of wrongs.

Love does not delight in evil but rejoices with the truth.

It always protects,
Always trusts,
Always hopes,
Always perseveres.
Love never fails.

This commitment requires that both partners in a marriage show up and do their part to make the relationship work.

Yes, there will be many times when every fiber within says "I don't want to do this." But the truth of a commitment is Love is not proud and you must persevere.

Love is about commitment.

There have been so many times when I too, wished I had been able to act on my "feelings." When you, as my mate did not provide as you said you would, I always had hope.

When you did not support or help build confidence, as you should have, I was patient.

I realize now that I was not as loving as I should have been. Because I was not committed to loving myself, I allowed unloving deeds to happen to all of us. Love does not dishonor others.

It took a while for me to understand what true love was all about. I can only take so much disregard for love from someone I love. The truth is that love is so easy to have but we have to be committed in order to follow the laws of love as given in the bible.

It became clear that I would never get the things I needed most from you. Your love, your compassion, your honesty and your integrity...and to think that you can give that freely if you wanted. You may never understand what true love entails.

Love is not about a feeling. It is a gift you give to those around you. Period.

ME AND YOU

I have almost closed the door
To the life I had with you
I can smile without regret
About the love I had for you
I sometimes miss the closeness of your skin
When I laid so close to you
If only things had stayed the same
As when I first fell in love with you

We must have blinked because one day
Things seemed to change between me and you
Tempers flared, voices raised
No understanding left for me and you
You felt trapped, I felt stuck
That was not good for me and you
You went away, I decided to stay
We could not live together as me and you

We tried to fix our scarred, worn, broken hearts
But the pieces no longer fit for me and you
Time together had run its course
That was to be for me and you

THE BREAK UP

We said goodbye, I know I cried

But I could no longer be me as me and you
Some happy memories of what we had
Are all I have left between me and you

I am sure you have closed the door
To your heart these days for me
That is how it has to be
So that you can be free from me
I know that there was once some joy we shared
Together, pleasant times holding me
But years can change many things
One can't explain to even me

Me and you, I guess we are done
Me and you, we really did have fun
Me and you, no longer live as one
Me and you

NO MORE LIES

Go to hell is what I yelled at him,
But the words never came out of my mouth
Although they rang loudly in my head.

I could not believe HE would stand there,
And tell me just to get over it.
Then he said, I did it and yes it happened.
I can't change what I have done
So YOU need to deal with this the best way you can.
Then he had the nerve to say, and furthermore we will
not discuss this again.

No mention of the simple phrase, I'm sorry,
No sound of remorse in his voice,
Just a crazy look on his face as he looked at me because
I dared to be mad as hell for his not caring enough to
protect the sacredness that was supposed to be based on
trust.

At that point, I did not know who was crazier, me or
him.
Then I snapped

Oh yes, I yelled
Go to hell...but this time the words sprang from my
mouth loud and clear and he heard it as the words rang
and lingered in the air
He was stunned as I looked him dead in the eye and
dared him to say something stupid,
anything that sounded like another lie.

Humf. No more lies mother fucker.

PS: Lord please forgive me for my foul mouth today.

SOMETIMES HE BUYS ME GRAPES

My very best friend had the nerve to say,

He doesn't do a thing for you

It's always about him, him, and him

Why do you stay?

 I looked at her

As she challenged me

Wanting me to stand up and see that I was holding on to

a hope that had seen better days

So in defense, I opened my mouth and belligerently

blurted out,

"Sometimes he buys me grapes."

That was all I could say,

That was the best that I could say.

I looked at her,

She looked at me

She rolled her eyes at me

Then with clenched teeth and a sarcastic tone in her

voice she asked,

"Were they seedless grapes or grapes with seeds? Were

they red grapes, green grapes or black grapes, because

you know it makes a difference.

Annoyed I said who the hell cares what kind of grapes
they were?
I looked at her
She looked at me
And we both burst out in uncontrollable laughter,
Because the only good thing I had to say about him
was....
Sometimes he buys me grapes

STUFF

It started off with his stuff
I also had my stuff
then all the stuff became
just our stuff
but some of our stuff
was only my stuff
and some of the stuff
was only his stuff

sometimes our attitudes would get kind of gruff
because we could not reconcile
what was between our stuff
things got messed up
we got mixed up
had some problems
over so much stuff

He said he was doing all this stuff
so that we would one day have enough
I said I don't want that other stuff
What you and I create can be enough
Strangely enough

what we have is good enough
if we try hard enough
to figure out this stuff

Then our personalities collided and started to bluff
this is not poker I said in a huff
The king and queen haggled and began to puff
all the hot air between them over all of this stuff

Things got so hot they had to part
to get a new start
that wasn't so smart
they found that their hearts
felt riddled with darts
It was quite a shame
and who is to blame

All that I know is it started with his stuff
Yes, I had my stuff
The truth is it never really became our stuff
As sad as it seems
It is the little things that get in the way
when stuff rules the day.

WATCHING TV —REALITY SHOW

We sat quietly
Staring at the TV
Me in my chair with the vibrating back, relaxed.
Him in his recliner, with his legs stretched out, relaxing
Waiting for each other to say something...
Neither of us dared to be the first to say anything
because if we did it would weaken our individual
position

I needed to hear him say, just once, I'm sorry
But all I heard was the blaring silence
that seemed to quiet the noise coming from the TV

He sat there looking at the TV as if he were in deep
thought
Every so often I would catch him taking a quick glance at
me.

I knew he wanted to say something,
But I dared not ask what was on his mind
So I waited patiently, to hear his words
He exhaled,

THE BREAK UP

But he never said a thing

We continued to sit quietly
Both staring at the TV
Me in my chair with the vibrating back, relaxed.
Him in his recliner, with his legs stretched out, relaxing

Maybe he was waiting for me to ask a question like
"How do we fix this?"
But I too, was silent

There we sat
Watching TV
Then the TV began to watch us
We were the stars in our own reality TV show,
The performance was Live.

It was a sad story
And the upcoming episode was not looking good.
What an unexpected twist of fate because it had such a
magical start

Just like a fairy tale
Once upon a time
Now it was falling apart while we watched TV

Quietly
Silently
Waiting
And then it was over.

We sat fixated
Staring at the TV
Me in my chair with the vibrating back.
Him in his recliner, with his legs stretched out.
The End

THE BREAK UP

Tears, anger, heartbreak ...I wish it didn't hurt so, but it does.

- "Why Does It Hurt So Bad" *by Whitney Houston*
- "I Can't Make You Love Me" *by Bonnie Raitt*
- "It's Too Late" *by Carol King*
- "Didn't We Almost Have It All" *by Whitney Houston*
- "Every Breath You Take" *by The Police*
- "Breaking Up Is Hard To Do" *by Neil Sedaka*
- "How Can You Mend a Broken Heart" *by The Bee Gees*

What song made you emotional after the break-up?

MOVING ON

A CUP OF TEA

I wanted a cup of tea
I looked in the canister where I store the open boxes of
tea bags
The only choices I had were Pomegranate Tea and
Raspberry Tea.
I don't care for either one of them.

.

Darn it!!!
I should not have purchased the assorted blend.
I knew I would be stuck with these two leftover blends,
and I am.

As I debated which one I could tolerate the best,
I stopped and decided I would have neither.
I have to stop settling for things I don't like.
Making do, when I don't have to make do

I filled my huge mug with boiling hot water,
added some fresh lemon juice and a little maple syrup
I gently stirred the mixture with my spoon,
Laid the spoon on the saucer and cupped both my hands
around my mug and I took a sip.

Moving On

Um-m-m...Have mercy.
This is just the way I like it.

Over the years settling has become a habit.
But with the major changes I have made in my personal
life
I no longer have to sacrifice all of my likes so that
everyone else can enjoy all that they like.

I am not blaming anyone for the predicament that
became my norm.

I put up with it so often,
that it became expected.
I allowed it to happen.

Some thought I was happy when everyone else around
me was happy.
I was,
but I wanted some of what they expected from me.
Not all the time, but every blue moon would have been
nice.
There were times I would cry out,

When is it my turn to have someone care about what I
like to do

I never got an answer.
Now, it is finally my turn to have a turn.

Wow
I am just not that used to having a turn
Now that it is my turn I choose to take it
It doesn't come easy
I am learning new ways of thinking, doing and being.
The doing is the most important thing.
I find as I do more of the things I like,
I touch and influence more people who also like what I
like

I think I'll have another cup of hot lemon tea with a
touch of maple syrup.
I do like it like that.

I HAVE BEEN CALLED

I had a little dream
I wanted so badly for me
The vision I had seen,
Was my future destiny

I shared this dream with others
Who looked quite surprised at me
And said that I was crazy
To even think that I could be

The person in that dream
 It most likely wasn't me
They said "You're just a little person
And that big dream could never be"

I pondered in my mind
If they knew me better than I knew me
If they had a special vision
Which I could not yet see

Then I thought about their dreams
That they never dared to share
And I got this funny feeling

That they wanted me to fail
And experience the same doom and gloom that showed
up as hurt which they wore just like a badge,
Due to disillusion
Influenced by somebody who dared to squash their
precious dream

A piece of them died as this enemy took away their hope
Then they walked away in anguish and the longing of
ambition began to slowly fade.
And in their pain they looked to me, and tried to impose
the same pain

Victim...oh no, not for me
I decided I that I was going to be free
Of someone else's impression
Of what my life should be

This is not an impulsive fling
It calls my name
It makes me sane
I find that I can no longer contain
My enthusiasm with

Moving On

This dog gone "thang"

So I leaped into action with focused integrity
Because....
I have a dream
That I know I will attain,
And yes I plan to serve you well,
With the fruits my toil will gain

But for now,
I want your silence, it will serve us both, I vow
You don't have to like my words or understand my how
Just don't judge my possibilities
As an unlikely probability
Because you have no idea of my real capabilities

But with time, at the right time
You will witness my cherished abilities.

So sit back, and relax
And let my dream alone.
It is my dream, and with my vision
I will be very clear
In my intention

To resolve another's tension
With my dream, because
I have been called.

FEAR

What do you do when
Fear comes knock, knock, knocking on your door
Do you close your eyes
Do you shiver and shake
Do you cry
Do you hide
Do you yell
Do you tell fear to wait
And if you do, does your fear go away when fear comes
knock, knock, knocking on your door.

If you shudder to think that Fear will return to visit you
once more.
You're not alone.
Fear has knocked on many doors.

Fear has visited me often and I used to hide
I used to pretend that fear was really my friend
Protecting me keeping me safe by telling me that I could
not do better
Convincing me that I needed to accept what I had and be
satisfied with that

Fear said my dreams were only make believe
Fear allowed me to stay trapped day after day
In a life that limited my choices
Because I was too afraid to open the door when fear
came to visit me

Then one day fear came knock, knock, knocking on my
door again
And much to my surprise
I took a deep breath
I gathered my resolve
I opened my eyes and what a surprise that I found.

Fear ran away when I opened the door when fear came
knock, knock, knocking on my door.

I NEVER KNEW HIM

Although ...I married him,

I never knew Him

I only saw the man I wanted him to be

I closed my eyes when my faith was saying leave him

please

I stayed thinking he would change, one day, someday for

me

He drew me in with dashing charm and cheerful laughter

Then turned his back when he caused nothing but

disaster

I tried to fix this situation

When he left me at the station

To find my way, those days were gray

I thought "I do" meant he would always treat me like I

was special

I prayed that love would mend the mental cruelty that

seemed to prevail

I felt alone

I was alone

But I wanted more than anything to have a home

I learned to play the game of "You can hide the shame"
I paid the bills, I worked in pain,
Yes I complained I needed help,
And he laughed and said
You need to accept the hand that you have been dealt

I wanted so much for us to be a WE
Instead everything was about pleasing HE
I lost my heart and almost lost my desire to be
Until the day he mistakenly set me free

It was quite by chance, No more song and dance
I asked "why do you stay"
He said "it's convenient this way"
I asked "where is the love"
He said, "that I got rid of"
I asked "what about the years"
He laughed and said, "It's just time you volunteered"

I'd been praying for a sign.
It had been there all the time
I just disobeyed the voice
That protects and guides one's choice
Free will, sometimes leads you through a maze

Moving On

But God's will, leads you to be amazed

Yes, I married him so that we would become one
But we were two and three and four and other sums
I know for sure that I never really got to meet,
The man who initially swept me off my feet
There was a door to his heart that I could not open
That led to feelings that left both of us so broken

Love is freedom and I needed to be free
So I broke the chains that had imprisoned me
He held the key to unlock his heart
But he could not see to share this part with even me

So I wish him well, as I say goodbye
I have no more tears to shed, so I can no longer cry
About the years I spent
In love with someone who chose to live alone within

I know that time
Will soothe this wound
I have some grace
And much to embrace

Yes, I will look for love

Again I am sure

I will never ever close that door.

IT TOOK ME A WHILE TO UNDERSTAND

It took me a while to understand
That sometimes pleasing a man
Means that he makes demands
That he thinks should improve where a woman stands...

You can't always trust what's in his eyes
Cause his true feelings, he often hides
The agenda which ultimately guides
The choices he makes during life's ride

He thinks he wants someone to fix
But soon realizes he must rewrite his script
It seems his heart will contradict
The terms he had when he was
Desiring to own a part of someone
He did not know would or could change

After all man's heart often leads him full steam ahead
Guided by his eyes and how it makes him feel
With that visual stimulation ruling his head
Telling him

If she listens, then maybe I will share my heart
Because she will have proven she might be worthy of the
part

What he doesn't understand, is that a woman is fine the
way she is
She is not broken baby,
 And you can't fix her on demand

LIFE IS COMPLICATED

Life is complicated.

When I met him he said he was separated.

I asked him what that meant?

He said his wife left him because they did not get along.

He had a son, whom he loved

But he was moving on,

Because they just could not seem to get it together.

I knew he cared for his wife,

I saw the hurt and the longing in his eyes, when he spoke

of her

But I also saw a kind man,

a sexy man,

ready to start again

with me.

We clicked and we fit together

But a separated man with a young son has issues

He really did not want another man raising his son

I admired that

He wondered what he could have done differently

Sometimes we talked about it

All of us have faults

Owning them and fixing them takes strength of
character.

Separation is funny.
Many times it is hard to let go even though you don't
want to be together.
Life is complicated.

I left him because if he came to me he would not be
whole.
His heart was still healing from separation
He understood what his responsibility was as a man.
I loved him even more.

I wanted to be with him.
He wanted to be with me
I didn't really want to leave him
If only I had met him before he said I do
This just was not our time, not now.
There were matters of the heart that still needed to be
resolved.

I moved on.
My heart ached.

Moving on

It was the right thing to do
Life is complicated.

REALITY FROM MY LAWYER

There are two sides to everything
One that is his and one that is hers
This is something we lawyers always observe
The funny thing is
When I hear each of the party's side,
I have to put my personal feelings aside
If I don't, all objectivity will soon disappear

Each of the stories should really be the same
But both of the stories are usually insane
At times I have to wonder
Was he or she even there
To witness the tales they now dare to share

Which one is right
Which one is wrong
My mind is playing a game of ping pong
As we stumble along

What of this makes sense,
To think this is only the start
My trying not to look shocked
Is such a good art

Moving On

I sit, listen and wonder how he or she dare
To share this sad story
its absurdity seems allegory

Oh-oh, let me catch myself
The subjectivity is now coming into play
I say sternly
What are the facts
I want only the facts
No excuses
No explanations
I just want the facts and that is that

I need to hear the whole truth
And nothing but the truth
Without that I cannot represent you well
It's all about the facts

Leave out the he said, she said or they did this or that.
All of that extra information is just a matter of fact
I do understand, I don't want to cross the line,
But feelings just don't matter in court most of the time

The components of both stories have to make sense,

Your perspective is just hindsight
Which may offer you some insight,
But probably not much light,
You have got to move on

Let's wrap this all up,
It has been a great start
I need time to decipher just what we've got
Discovery will uncover items which are unclear
But understand man's law is not necessarily fair.

I don't make the rules,
I just do the best that I can
To help you resolve this unfortunate affair

MOVING ON

RICHARD CAN HOWL

As a lady I must choose my words wisely
When it comes to discussing matters that are frowned
upon
So I will use the word "Richard"
when I mean the word "dick."

I just didn't want community "Richard"
Knocking on my door
thinking was I willing to accept his "Richard" anymore
I heard it had been poking into places where it never
should have been
And when I asked him was this true he smiled with such
a stupid grin

This "Richard" thought that everyone should have a tasty
treat
and that his "Richard" should be willing to be the
sacrificial piece
cause the ladies, if you call them that
would be willing and begging for more
 of this magical thing called "Richard"
At least that is what he swore

That may be true for
Some who have desires much different than my own
So I told this "Richard" to take his "Richard" to
somebody else's home

I said, "Richard" I understand you think that you must
use it before you lose it
but you've confused that little thing
by poking your little "Richard" everywhere trying to
make it sing
All over the community leaving havoc everywhere
Now you're crying that "Richard" wants to come home
because it is a cold cruel world out there

"Richard" said he understands that he was a-wagging
where the other dogs bow-wowed
And his ego got a boost as the other dogs all howled
To the moon, in unison and very much in tune
Then they ran off like the barking hounds they were
With their tails tucked between their hind legs

Then there stood this "Richard" alone without his
howling dogs

They understood much better than this "Richard" every
would
That community "Richard" had been up to no good.
Now, he was about to lose his home.
All the howling dogs prayed that "Richard" would find a
new bone.
Bow-wow,
Ruff-ruff.

REGINA GALE

THE DISAPPOINTMENT OF MY FAILURE

The disappointment of my failure
To make you love me well
Is subsiding, and I find that
I am no longer crying

I'm not finding ways to blame you
For hurting me so deep,
Because it was easier to hurt me
Than to face your own pains which caused you distress
beyond belief

It is not my failure that disappoints me
Regret is for the relationship we shared
Now broken beyond repair

Where was the true conviction,
That allowed lustful competition
To destroy revered expectations between us

How could the tenderness of love
not be enough to see that I was always there

Moving on

Wanting to hold on to you because I cared

How could I know
That it was easier to hurt me
Than it was to deal with what was hurting you

This relationship was not a failure
But it was a disappointment
Because our love was worth the fight
Of holding on
Of being strong until that day
I lost all hope
When you turned to say you did not care
You said you had no memories with me you cared to
share
It was as if I was never even there
I was not in your heart, you said to me.
You had no love to give to me
Just wasted years, so many years being washed away
This time I heard it when you said just let it go
I said ok, as a melancholy rage
Began to stir
Disappointment with my failure of trying to force a love

Even though I knew that one can never demand
another's love
I can no longer pretend that we are devoted to the end
I understand
After all it is easier to hurt me
Than it is to face that thing that is hurting you

I know what love is like
And now I demand it to be a part of my life
That will require someone who finds it hard to hurt me
Even when they are hurting inside
They still will love me freely
And show me by their actions that they care about
Our commitment to be one
Our desire to be together
Our trust that no one is allowed to pierce

I will then be strong enough to weather the storm
That my love may be going through
Even when he is hurting inside
Because he will love me well and I will love him well
And I will let nothing destroy what we both protect
A real love,

Moving on

A true love would never hurt me
Even if he, my love was hurting,
and the love I give to him could not kiss his hurt away.
I may only be able to make his hurt easier to bear, but I
will be there
Together we will work through any disappointment
We will know that our love is never a failure
It will just be Love

I know it was just easier for you to hurt me
than deal with your pain.
Through it all, I learned what to demand from myself in
love,
from my disappointment of my failure with you.

MOVING ON

Sometimes you have no choice but to move on.
You are in charge of you now.
Here are 7 songs that share some meaning for where you are at this time in your journey.

- "Since You Been Gone" *by Kelly Clarkson*
- "Cry Me A River" *by Julie London*
- "Just Don't Wanna Know" *by Marvin Winans*
- "I Can Let Go Now" *by Michael McDonald*
- "I Believe I Can Fly" *by R. Kelly*
- "It's My Turn" *by Diana Ross*
- "I Will Survive *by Gloria Gaynor*

Did I pick anything that had a meaning for you if you are moving on?

BACK TO ME

A SEED

So often one discounts the gifts
That are uniquely theirs
Ways that come so easily
With very little care

You were born with unknown grace
Presented as a seed
The little seed inside of you will one day be a tree
If nurtured and tended carefully
Your fruit will feed many needs
But understand your fruit is one of a kind
Be it bitter, be it sweet

Sometimes you will observe that jealous eyes
Will try to cut down your fruitful tree
They will break your limbs and pick the fruit
Before the harvest can begin

Oh unique one please be strong
You can survive the dreadful drought
Believe that your seed is resilient enough
It is endowed by nature's loving touch

You are like no other tree
Your foundation must be solid
To realize the special fruits
That will help others, also, grow strong

Never discount your talents
Whatever they may be
The value you will bring to those
Will be lost if you can't see
That the simple little seed you are will one day be a tree.

FREE WILL

Free me from my free will
That is what I sometimes pray
My independent choices
Mean that trouble is on the way

I start with good intentions
That point we can debate
I get blinded by the process
While forgetting what should be weighed

What is the desired intention
Can there be a better way
Am I repeating all the basic steps
That should be fixed along the way

Lest I forget
That I am the one
Who is in control
Of what is to be
Of my destiny
Which directly leads
To my legacy
I must appreciate

The power provided me
Through
Free will.

I AM A COMPLEX WOMAN

I'm a complex woman,
God made me this way
I am magnificent in every way
From the sound of my voice
To the heart within my frame
I am unique and cannot be contained

I understand that all you may see
Is the roundness of my hips,
The hair-do that I wear.
The way I stride when I pass by
Sometime you may wonder why
Some things make me cry
But this is because of the way I have been designed

I bring life into this world
I laugh when people say I'm just a girl
I am a she and am proud to be
I am a queen, and I rule many things
When you walk into the palace that I sometimes share
with a king
You will find that I am the supporting neck which allows
his head to be

BACK TO ME

Yes, I am complex
You must agree
And every woman is as complex as I see me
I am unique
You must also agree
That every "she" was made in perfection
Though imperfect by selection
Of someone who does not value the riches which can
come

If you listen closely to the sound of my voice
You will soon find the ways to make me rejoice
And when I am happy you will find
That everything you want will be divine
Because, I am a complex woman,
I was made that way
God designed me in perfection
In every way.

I SHOWED UP

Sometimes we think that life is not fair,
It's true and no one really cares
Except you, and you know what you should do
Is suspend the voices that give you the blues

It starts with just a change of heart
A desire to step into the part
That calls out to you and captivates your soul
And allows you to now be bold

You release the fear that threatens your soul
You rekindle the things that once made you whole
You rely on your faith and believe
that which you seek is yours
if you dare to relinquish some peeps
Who have no dreams or desires of which they can tell.
So they try to take your dreams and send them to hell

Because you love them, you make a deal with yourself
To distance your love and heal with some help
You take a step forward then open the door
And with much surprise you see that there is so much
more

Ahead of you, life is calling your name
Offering choices that will bring you acclaim

What did you do?
You decided in life that you would show up.

LOVE IS ALL I NEED

I tried to give you all of me
But you did not care to even see
that all I ever wanted from you was love, to be loved, to
feel loved and to know love from you.

Your love was wrapped around your sex
It did not spread into your chest where your heart beats
strong
but no part of it longs for real love, which requires that
you give love to have love to go on.

One day I could stand no more of this
Empty promises which left me expecting and deserving
bliss
from a man I loved and tried to make love me, so that we
would share a love that would last an eternity

Now my bed is empty, but my heart is strong
The joy I feel is balanced by the sadness of what is gone
The fairy tale ending for us will never be because
I deserve to feel love,
With a love that is an everlasting love
Which unselfishly lavishes love on me

because...
I always needed to be loved, and feel love
from the man I love, because
love is all I need

MY HAIR

I have gone and cut my hair
And now my head is almost bare
You may look at me and wonder
What caused me to make this major blunder

To retire my crown and glory
This must be a juicy story
Because vanity would never
Let a scissor clip whatever

Everyone knows that one's hair
Can hide many things
And even help to cure a little despair
It can change a look with just a swoop
Please add some gel to keep it there

Heaven forbid
A wind or rain
To cause my hairstyle
To fall and wane

Then one day,
When I needed to look my best

BACK TO ME

A blithering storm put me to the test
Nature's simple act betrayed the way
I handled my hair
That frightful bad hair day

I realized I had become a slave
To the idea that I needed a permanent wave.

I've had hair down my back
Piled high on my head,
Hair full of braids
And many other ways,
Hair parted on the left, on the right, down the middle
Bangs to the eyebrows
With curly locks a flowing
Dipping here and dipping there

I have worn wigs and weaves
And parts and things
To enhance what nature could not achieve

So I decided that bad hair day
To cut it off and see what laid

Beneath that crown and glory that I have always
depended on
I dared to see what I looked like in my rawest form

And I was surprised to see
That I would like this look for me
This natural look upon my head
Is peach fuzz soft,
Wiry and wild
With tiny curls of gray, white, silver and black
It is rather cute and that's a fact

I am as natural as I will ever be
And to think I almost let vanity
Not allow me to see
The real beauty of me being me

Yes, I have gone and cut my hair
And my head is almost bare
Now, when you look at me in wonder
You will know this is no blunder
Because I can truly share
That I am definitely not my hair

NO MORE

I woke up this morning and the first thing that popped
into my mind was
No more.
At the time, I did not know what that meant
All I knew was that no more was important to me...
These two small words that would rule my day.
No more will I remain involved with someone who has
not learned to love me with all their heart as I have loved
them, no more...
No more will I shed a tear behind the truth that remains
a secret because their omission of fact, is really a fact...no
more
No more will I wonder why the person who said they
would be there for me is never there for me...no more
No more will I pray alone, stand alone, be alone when I
am not alone...no more
No more will I doubt me because someone else chooses
not to see me...no more
Yes, I woke up this morning and the first thing that
popped into my mind, was no more.
I love no more.
Yes, two small words that ruled my day, today.
No more.

STOP

Stop hiding behind your guilt

It causes problems for your life

Speak the truth in love

Do the right thing, because

There is no need to disown one's imperfections

In order to play up to others, perceptions

Of who you should be

Don't worry.

It's who you think you are that needs to be addressed.

Are you genuine to yourself?

Are you holding secrets that have you trapped in a place

That offers you no freedom

Ensnared..., living someone else's dream

If so,

Stop!!

Regroup

The emptiness that is filling you up

Is as distasteful to you as it is to others

Don't concern yourself about not having all the answers

Seek the information

Have the heart to implement your reason for being

BACK TO ME

Live to share your experiences
Good and bad, good or bad
Be kind to your self
Be true
To you

You are awesome... let your light shine. It will brighten up everyone around you.

Here are some songs that can inspire the arrival of yourself to yourself. Welcome home.

- "Good Times" *by Chic*
- "Brave" *by Sara Bareilles*
- "I'm Every Woman" *by Chaka Khan*
- "Independent Women" *by Destiny's Child*
- "Video" *by India Aire*
- "Control" *by Janet Jackson*

Get up and dance to the music!!! Oh yea!!!

ABOUT THE AUTHOR

Regina is one of three daughters and four sons born to Winnie and Al Johnson. That fact alone connected her to binding family relationships as a sister, granddaughter, niece, cousin and other connected relations close and distant. Regina went on to become a friend to others and as years passed she became a girlfriend and a lover to a few.

Along the way Regina has been employed by small companies and major conglomerates that needed her many special and varied skills where she worked independently, managed teams, was and is a lifelong student, teacher, singer, and volunteer. Regina expanded her scope and became a working wife, while obtaining a graduate degree and juggled being a mom.

Over time Regina became extremely proficient at being a jack of all trades, by necessity. When asked what this was like and what she wants now, she shared:

"I was so busy being everything to everyone I forgot to be anything meaningful to myself. There was a void in my life and I almost forgot about the soul of me.

I was moving much too fast down the road so life punctured my wheels and caused me to step on the brakes. This brought me to a complete halt. It was only then that I allowed myself to look out of the window at my life and see the truth as it was then and as it is now. It hurt for a while and then it got better.

My journey prepared me to be able to share experiences that are not just mine. Some of these experiences are yours too. You will feel them, because you have lived them.

I have lived a very good life and I plan to live an even better one as I move forward in my "seasoned" years.

I am going to sing and dance as often as I can because it makes me feel good.

I'm going to love better than I have and play more than I have allowed myself to do in the past.

I am happier than I have been in a long time and for that I am extremely grateful.

Lemons are one of my favorite fruits. I love them...especially the soft skinned variety. This bitter fruit is tasty as is, but when you add a little sugar and some water you create something deliciously sweet and refreshing.

That is what our lives should be, refreshing. We must take the bitter and do what we must to make it sweet, and refreshing."

REGINA GALE

BONUS GIFT REMINDER

The conversation continues with your free gift.

Reflections of Love,

a chapbook, is offered for sale but **is a special gift to you.**

Go to
http://www.sometimeshebuysmegrapes.com/ROLbook
to register for your gift

You will find monthly updates that will be available to you that are created to make you smile and improve the quality of your life. We only get one chance at life; let's do all we can to make it a good life.

Always,
Regina Gale